To the Beautiful Couple

FOR THE NEWLY ENGAGED COUPLE,
THE NEWLY MARRIED COUPLE,
AND THOSE WHO HAVE BEEN MARRIED FOR YEARS.
THIS IS FOR YOU.

FOREVER AFTER
Published by LHC Publishing 2022

Text Copyright © 2022 Y. Eevi Jones
Illustrations Copyright © 2022 Y. Eevi Jones
Cover Design by Y. Eevi Jones
Cover Art by Anna Ismagilova

Printed in the USA.

All the characters in this book are fictitious, and any resemblance to actual persons living or dead is purely coincidental.

All rights reserved. No part of this publication may be reproduced, distributed, or transmitted in any form or by any means, or stored in a database or retrieval system, without the prior written permission of the copyright holder.

All inquiries should be directed to
www.LHCpublishing.com

ISBN-13: 978-1-952517-15-0 Paperback
ISBN-13: 978-1-952517-14-3 Hardcover

Life's Biggest Moments
FOREVER AFTER

For Newlyweds and Engaged Couples

WRITTEN BY
EEVI JONES

And So it Begins:

When two worlds have turned into one,
where a *Forever*'s no longer enough;
that's when tummies filled with butterflies
have blossomed fully into true love.

You promise each other the moon and the stars,
the world, and the skies up above.
You dance through the night and plan for a life
that's filled with hope, compassion, and love.

May today be the day that's remembered
as the day you both became one.
May today be the day where you both will begin
your new lives at the onset of dawn.

Whatever the future may bring,
no matter how tough or how bold,
decide to conquer together
whatever each day may hold.

There is no love too big.
So don't fear to love a lot.
Don't hold back and be afraid
to love with all you've got.

Love fully thrives and blossoms
when your promises made are kept true.
For each upheld promise grows stronger the trust –
in each other, your bond, and in you.

Travel the globe and explore lands afar.
Get inspired by the new.
Embracing adventures together,
you both grow a world's well-rounded view.

Give time and space to one another.
Spend days in twos AND on your own.
Have the happiest of laughter
be the soundtrack of your home.

Conversations 'bout your day,
'bout your dreams, your hopes, your fear -
make those the moments you both treasure.
Make those the moments you hold dear.

Appreciate each other
every day anew.
Remind yourself of what your bond
truly means to you.

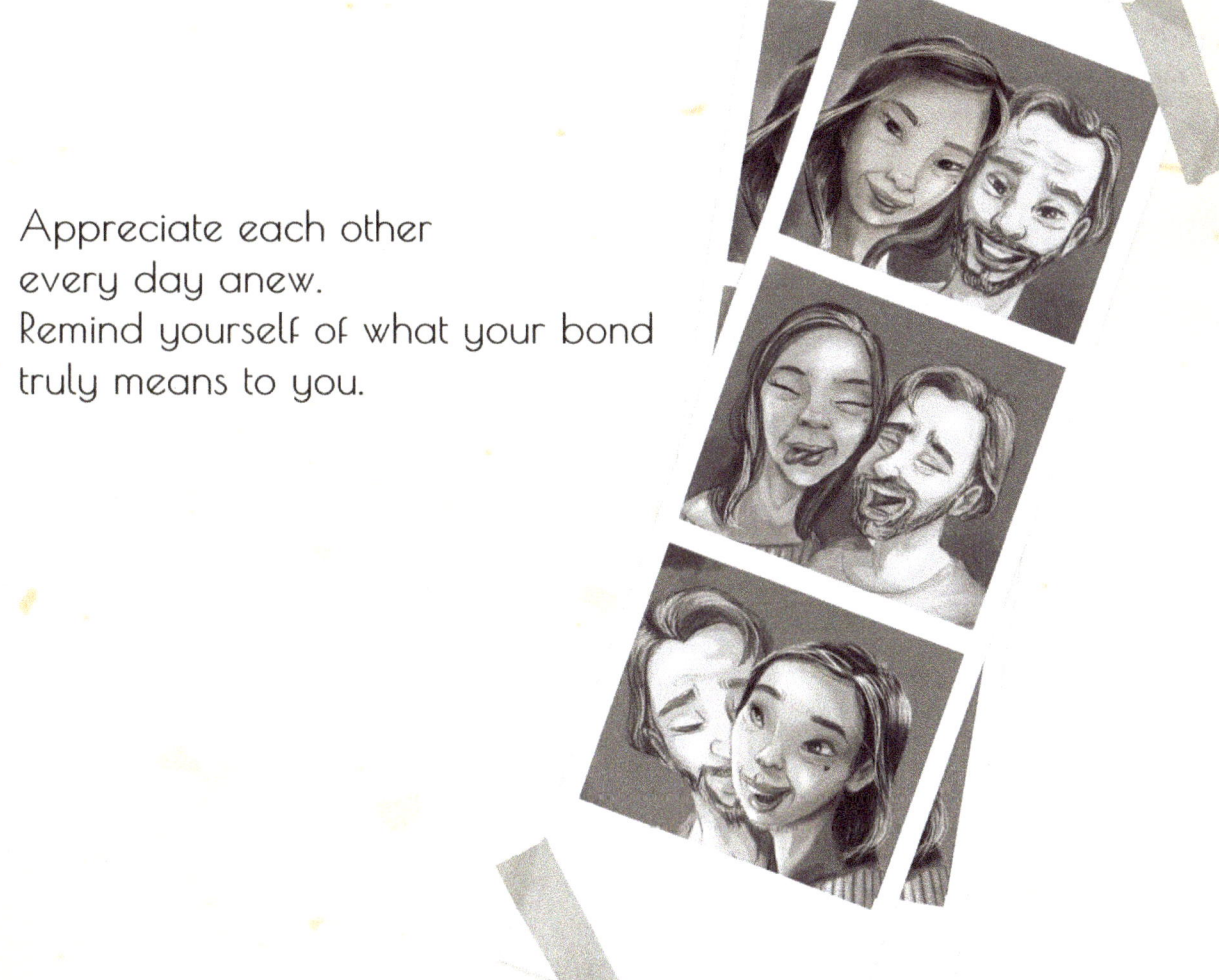

See the best in one another;
each others' good and heart.
That's how you thrive together;
growing stronger, not apart.

Love means respect, appreciation.
For one another. A give and take.
Love means passion, smiles, forgiving
of mistakes you both will make.

It's so easy to love each other
when things – they all go right.
But times that count the most of all
are those where you must fight.

Fight through thick and thin.
Through hardships and distress.
Where despite opposing views
you're supportive nonetheless.

What seems so big today,
tomorrow, it may not.
So don't pick battles that don't matter
over things that do a lot.

Love, it is a choice
you'll have to make anew each day.
Where saying yes to one another
decides what lasts or fades away.

So CHOOSE to love each other;
be it sun or rain or snow;
in good times and in bad;
in times of ebb and flow.

For love is a commitment,
not just a feeling that we feel.
It's the loving nonetheless,
despite times far from ideal.

May your hearts beat for each other
with adoration and love so true,
that every day with confidence
you say 'I do' anew.

You now both get to share a new life
that's filled with love and laughter.
You now both get to live your dream
of a happy *Forever After.*

ABOUT THE AUTHOR

Writing under a number of pen names, Eevi Jones is a USA Today & WSJ bestselling and award-winning author and ghostwriter of children's books.

Born in former East Germany to a German mother and a Vietnamese father, Eevi loves to infuse her children's books with racial diversity. She is the founder of Children's Book University where dreams really do come true. "Life's Biggest Moments" is Eevi's first series for adults.

Eevi has been featured in media outlets such as Forbes, Scary Mommy, Business Insider, Huffington Post, and Exceptional Parent Magazine, and lives near D.C. with her husband and two boys.

She can be found online at www.BravingTheWorldBooks.com.

A WORD BY THE AUTHOR

Whether you are a newly engaged couple, a newly married couple, or have been married for many years, I hope that with this book you come to see how special and unique your bond truly is. May you create the most beautiful memories with one another, forging your very own FOREVER AFTER.

If this book touched you in any way, it would mean the world to me if you would take a short moment to leave a heartfelt review. Thank you.

OTHER WORKS BY THIS AUTHOR

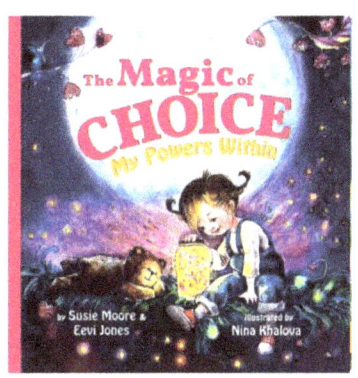 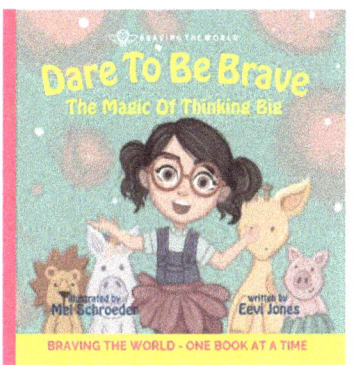 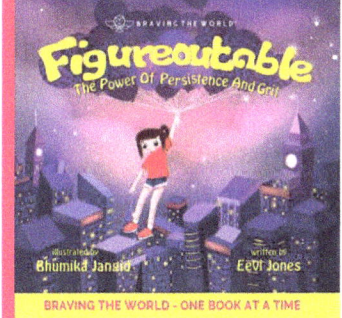

... AND MANY MORE

www.ingramcontent.com/pod-product-compliance
Lightning Source LLC
Chambersburg PA
CBHW040001290426
43673CB00077B/300